YOU
SHALL
DECREE

SHERRIE SALTZGABER

YOU SHALL DECREE

Commanding Your Crisis into Alignment
with the Word of God Through Prayer

LIFEWISE BOOKS

YOU SHALL DECREE

COMMANDING YOUR CRISIS INTO ALIGNMENT WITH THE WORD OF GOD THROUGH PRAYER

SHERRIE SALTZGABER

Copyright © 2023 Sherrie Saltzgaber. All rights reserved. Except for brief quotations for review purposes, no part of this book may be reproduced in any form without prior written permission from the author.

Unless otherwise noted, all scriptures are taken from the NEW INTERNATIONAL VERSION (NIV): Scripture taken from THE HOLY BIBLE, NEW INTERNATIONAL VERSION ®. Copyright© 1973, 1978, 1984, 2011 by Biblica, Inc.™. Used by permission of Zondervan

Scriptures marked ESV are taken from the THE HOLY BIBLE, ENGLISH STANDARD VERSION (ESV): Scriptures taken from THE HOLY BIBLE, ENGLISH STANDARD VERSION ® Copyright© 2001 by Crossway, a publishing ministry of Good News Publishers. Used by permission.

Scriptures marked NAS are taken from the NEW AMERICAN STANDARD (NAS): Scripture taken from the NEW AMERICAN STANDARD BIBLE®, copyright© 1960, 1962, 1963, 1968, 1971, 1972, 1973, 1975, 1977, 1995 by The Lockman Foundation. Used by permission.

Scriptures marked NKJV are taken from the NEW KING JAMES VERSION (NKJV): Scripture taken from the NEW KING JAMES VERSION®. Copyright© 1982 by Thomas Nelson, Inc. Used by permission. All rights reserved.

Scriptures marked TPT are taken from THE PASSION TRANSLATION®. Copyright © 2017, 2018, 2020 by Passion & Fire Ministries, Inc. Used by permission. All rights reserved. ThePassionTranslation.com.

Published by:

LIFEWISE BOOKS
PO BOX 1072
Pinehurst, TX 77362
LifeWiseBooks.com

To contact the author: SherrieSaltzgaber.com

IBSN Print – 978-1-958820-36-0
IBSN Ebook – 978-1-958820-37-7

DEDICATION

First and foremost, this book is dedicated to Holy Spirit. You are essential in guiding and leading us into understanding, appreciation, and implementation of Scripture.

In loving memory of Gracen Faith Saltzgaber and Aliyah Faith Saltzgaber, you have taught us more about faith and the loving heart of God in your short time here on earth than any other situation or circumstance we have experienced. We are forever grateful for your brief but powerful time with us. We long for the day we are reunited in Christ.

And to Adelynn Hope Saltzgaber, all one pound, three ounces of you taught us to live in greater measures of standing on and believing in and for the promises and words of God to manifest here on earth as it is in heaven. Your tenacious will to live and fierce spirit inspire us all to greater depths of faith in every word that comes forth from the mouth of God.

Finally, to all of our grandchildren, may you always know the love and faithfulness of Jesus as the cornerstone of your life. May the Word of God be the lamp unto your feet and the light unto your pathway all of your days. Walk in the presence and power of God through the Holy Spirit in your generation. You are world changers for the glory of God!.

CONTENTS

From the Heart of the Author	1
Introduction	5
1. Stand and Declare	9
2. Possible with God	11
3. Creator God	13
4. His Ways Are Higher	15
5. The Lord is Your Keeper	17
6. Kingdom Come	19
7. Your Word	21
8. Be Gracious	24
9. Stand	27
10. Rest in His Shadow	29
11. Cadence of Heaven Touching Earth	32
12. Significance of Numbers	35
13. All Hope	39
14. Blood of the Lamb	43
15. He Hears Us	47
16. No Greater Love	50
17. No God, but Jesus!	54
18. Mighty to Save	57

19. Peaceful Habitation	60
20. Perfect Peace	63
21. Found Faithful	66
22. With Us	68
23. Praiseworthy	71
24. Steadfast Not Shaken	74
25. Healing Wings	77
26. Just One Touch	80
27. Watchmen on the Wall	83
28. Sovereign	86
29. Face of God	89
30. Remember	92
31. At the Sound	95
32. Call You Blessed	98
33. He Will Keep You	101
34. Everlasting Covenant	104
35. Inherit the Land	107
36. Wait for the Lord	111
37. As an Olive Tree	113
38. Fearless	116
39. He Delights in You	119
40. Forty to Forty-One	121
41. Abound in Hope	124

42. His Greatness	127
43. Songs of Praise	131
44. Well with Your Soul	133
45. You Are	135
46. Victorious One	138
47. Beyond Measure	141
48. Established in Promise	144
49. Arm of the Lord	146
50. Jehovah Rapha	148
About the Author	151
Endnotes	153

FROM THE HEART OF THE AUTHOR

This book is not an invitation to use Scripture like a genie bottle to wish for your own desired outcome to any given circumstance. It is, however, an invitation to a lifelong partnership and dependency on every word and promise God has spoken through the *logos,* which is the written Word of God, and *rhema,* which is revelatory, Holy Spirit inspired Word of God.

I never intended to write a book of decrees because there are numerous decree books out there. But as life would have it, through much prodding from others who have asked for copies of the daily decrees I wrote while on our personal journey through crisis, I hesitantly consented to compile some of the decrees into book form.

This is my attempt to put a resource into the hands of others that can be used anytime but especially during the most vulnerable and weak moments in life. My prayer is that these written declarations might bring comfort, strength, and truth to you quickly, and they increase your ability to hang onto and grow in faith in the midst of crisis.

When I sensed the Lord asking me to write and share the decrees in this book, we were facing our own family crisis. In February of 2021, our precious twin granddaughters were born at twenty-three weeks. Aliyah Faith weighed in at less than a pound and Adelynn Hope weighed one pound and three ounces.

The medical team did not give much chance of hope for them to thrive or even live. As we began to pray and declare the Word of God over them, it was very quickly evident that God's kindness and mercy for Aliyah was to take her home to be with Him. Several hours after birth, Aliyah was in the arms of Jesus, experiencing nothing but perfect love, as in an instant, she was completely healed and in the actual presence of her Creator.

Our focus turned to Adelynn and all that God desired to do in her tiny life. We shifted the prayers and decrees to battle for all God spoke about healing and her destiny according to the very Word of God.

Please know that whenever we are praying for healing and for the miracle of God to intervene on our behalf for deliverance and wholeness, we walk in tension. This tension is between God's desires and His command to pray for all Jesus purchased on the cross regarding healing and the reality that things don't always turn out the way we pray. Through hearts of faith and hope, we pray and declare while we keep an open hand, making room for His ultimate decisions of love, mercy, and sovereignty. He alone knows best.

God commands us to pray for the sick. At this moment, it is not time for timidity or shrinking back but rather to pray as children of God, contending for miracles, and we will do so with everything in us as we partner with heaven over life, wholeness, and health.

With our very last breath, we will declare, fight, and stand, believing on the very words of God for whatever situation we find ourselves in while ultimately trusting His ways when they are not our ways. We are responsible to pray and declare what the Lord is saying; the outcome belongs to God.

We are called to live in faith by believing God and His Word. 2 Corinthians 5:7 tells us we walk by faith not by sight. What or whom we believe is the bedrock of the foundation for our lives. Choosing to believe God over circumstances will always be met by God, Himself. God is attracted to faith. The kingdom of God operates through faith.

In Numbers 13-15, we read the account of twelve leaders being sent to bring back a report. Joshua and Caleb saw beyond what their natural senses experienced, and they, by faith, believed what God had spoken to them. The other ten leaders chose to believe what their natural senses took in through the facts they experienced, and this created two very different outcomes. Ten died in their unbelief, and the other two experienced the evidence of their faith in the fulfillment of what God spoke.

I strongly encourage you to go read these chapters for yourself. The point I want to make is that believing God, taking Him at His word, and declaring it out loud matters. What we believe impacts not only our own life but the lives of our descendants. God wants those who will take Him at His word and make a choice to stand, no matter what, in believing for God's Word to be fulfilled.

I, for one, have determined in my heart to believe God for greater things. I believe these declarations of faith will be a valuable and powerful resource in your arsenal of weapons as you face the battles ahead. I encourage you to become the mighty warrior, armed and ready as the victor God has destined you to be.

INTRODUCTION

OPEN YOUR MOUTH

"You will also decree a thing, and it will be established for you; And light will shine on your ways" Job 22:28 (NAS). A decree is defined as "a formal and authoritative order having the force of law; a judicial decision or order, to command, ordain or decide by decree."[1] It is not enough to just read the Word of God or to know about the Word of God. We, by faith, must determine we are settled on the side of believing what God has said in His Word. "I will declare the [Lord's] decree…" Psalm 2:7 (NKJV).

According to Hebrews 11:1, faith is the substance, the reality of what we hope for. This substance called faith is evidence of things we cannot yet see. In Matthew 19:26, Jesus, Himself, makes this statement, "…with God all things are possible," and again in Mark 9:23 (NKJV), "…all things are possible to him who believes." I'm not going to go too deep into these two statements except to say that through faith, the things that seem impossible through our human lens are often made possible through Christ for those who choose to believe what God says about the matter. From beginning to end, the Bible emphasizes the vitally important role faith plays in our relationship with Jesus and the kingdom of God.

Hebrews 11:3 (NAS) says, "By faith we understand that the worlds were prepared by the word of God, so that what is seen was not made out of things which are visible." There is a contrast in this verse between visible, (what we can see and experience with our natural senses) and that which is invisible (unseen with the natural senses).

Our natural senses help us connect with the tangible, visible world around us and the facts and circumstances we are faced with. Faith connects us to the invisible, unseen, underlying reality of the Word of God that holds all things together. Faith is connected to God and His Word. Paul teaches us that faith and sight are often in opposition to each other. 2 Corinthians 5:7 (NKJV) says, "For we walk by faith, not by sight."

One of my favorite Bible verses for much of my walk with Jesus is Psalm 27:13 (NAS). This is where David said, "I would have despaired unless I had believed that I would see the goodness of the LORD in the land of the living." Look at the order of that statement, the world around us tries to convince us that "seeing is believing." Not so for the one who claims to be a child of God. I am reminded of another statement Jesus made to His friend Martha, "Did I not say to you, if you believe, you will see the glory of God?" (John 11:39-40).

Jesus is still asking the same question to those of us who are His children. We must believe we will see. We do not see first, then believe. We believe what God has said first, then, as a result of standing on the Word of God, we see. Faith comes before sight.

We live in the tension between faith and sight. Our old nature or "flesh" desires and is most comfortable with the use of our senses. It often demands to see first. I, for one, want to grow and cultivate my "new man" or new nature that is able to trust God at His word without demanding immediate evidence or seeing before I am willing to believe Him.

This place of growth does not just happen on its own. It takes daily intentionality and purposeful action on my part to engage and cooperate with Holy Spirit and the Word of God as I experience life. To live from this place of belief, we must desire to grow in the character, actions, and nature as imitators of Jesus. Jesus lived completely dependent on every word that flowed from the Father.

One word from God can change everything. It can change our family trajectory, our health, our future, our finances, and our atmosphere. When we agree with what God says and choose to verbalize in faith what He is saying, we will see the purposes and promises of our faithful God fulfilled.

> "...*Open your mouth with a mighty decree; I will fulfill it now, you'll see! The words that you speak, so shall it be!*"
> Psalm 81:10 (TPT)

We are told in Scripture that our words are powerful, so much so that they can lead to life or death, according to Proverbs 18:21. God doesn't just want any old words coming out of our mouths. He wants His words coming forth. Why? Because He said, "The words that I speak to you are spirit, and they are life" (John 6:63 NKJV). Everyone who has proclaimed Jesus as Lord needs to understand that God longs to put His words upon our lips to be spoken from our mouths.

I am reminded of a story from Jeremiah 1:9-10 (NKJV), "Then the LORD put forth His hand and touched my mouth, and the LORD said to me: 'Behold, I have put My words in your mouth. See, I have this day set you over the nations and over the kingdoms, to root out and to pull down, to destroy and to throw down, too build and too plant.'"

God has not changed His desire of putting His words in the mouths of His people for the purposes of operating in the authority He gives to His children to root out, pull down, destroy, build, and plant. They do this by the power God grants His people. God's words in the mouth of His people are a powerful force to be reckoned with. This force can bring healing to the sick, freedom to the captive and prisoner, strength to the weary and weak, hope to the hopeless, and eternal life to all who believe.

The decrees in the pages ahead are samples of alignment with the Word of God. There is nothing magical in the words themselves, but as you seek Holy Spirit and agree with the words of God, declaring from your mouth the truths of His Word over your circumstances, be prepared to experience the presence and power of God.

DECREE ONE
STAND AND DECLARE

God, you said we would stretch out our hands to heal and that signs miracles and wonders would be performed in the mighty name of Jesus (Acts 4:30).

Jesus, you told us to ask for, walk in, and expect signs and wonders to manifest here on earth as it is in heaven, or they would not believe us (John 4:48). We are those who believe You. We are declaring the faith and belief of the Body of Christ to rise higher because You are releasing evidence of who You are as miracle, creator God (Matthew 17:20).

I decree that I believe nothing concerning _____ is impossible for You to accomplish. I am standing on Your words in Acts 3:16.

You said, by faith in Jesus's name, You make_____ strong, and faith through Jesus has given _____ perfect health in the presence of everyone.

So today, I declare from Acts 14:30, I will steadfastly remain standing and declaring boldly, speaking on behalf of the Word and grace of God, by our hands signs, miracles, and wonders shall be done.

_____, you shall live, thrive, and worship the Lord God Almighty with all your heart, mind, and body.

In Jesus' name, amen.

PRAYER:

_____

_____

_____

_____

PRAISES:

_____

_____

_____

_____

DECREE TWO
POSSIBLE WITH GOD

Jesus, You told Your disciples that with people things may be impossible but not so with God, for You said, "All things are possible with God" (Mark 10:27). I am declaring the power of God over the life of _____. What seems impossible with man is possible with God (Genesis 18:14).

Father, I confess this seems difficult, but nothing is too difficult for You. I believe that at Your appointed time, _____ will rejoice in the works You have performed. I acknowledge the limitations of man and declare the surpassing greatness of power that belongs to You alone. I put no confidence in anything but You, God (2 Corinthians 4:7).

God, I know You can do all things, and I wholeheartedly believe that no purpose of Yours can be thwarted in the life of _____ (Job 42:2). I receive the double portion blessing of the favor of the Lord.

Father, I speak a blessing over _____ today and call them blessed. You have commanded them to be fruitful and multiply so they could become a company of people declaring Your greatness (Genesis 28:3).

You alone, God, are the mighty One, and You have done great things for me. Holy is Your name (Luke 1:49). I believe You are in our midst, and You are a victorious warrior. You are rejoicing over _____ with shouts of joy (Zephaniah 3:17).

I declare, King Jesus is Lord over _____. I ask for the healing, living waters of Jesus to continuously flow, providing all nourishment and health to every part of _____'s body in Jesus' name!

PRAYER:

_____

_____

_____

PRAISES:

_____

_____

_____

DECREE THREE
CREATOR GOD

God, not only have You created _____'s inmost being but You are still creating it just as You knit them together in their mother's womb (Psalm 139).

Their frame is not hidden from You, for You are making them in the secret place. We praise You for this time in the sacred place that only Your eyes have seen and know what You are forming together for their good.

We declare that all the days You have ordained and decreed for _____ are written in Your book of life (Psalm 139:16).

_____, you will proclaim, "the Spirit of God has made me, and the breath of the Almighty gives me life" (Job 33:4). And on the basis of faith in His name, it is Jesus who has strengthened you, whom you see and know, and the faith that comes through Him has given you perfect health in the presence of all (Acts 3:16).

We declare, heal, O Lord, and they will be healed; save them, and they will be saved, for You, God, are the One we praise!

PRAYER:

PRAISES:

DECREE FOUR
HIS WAYS ARE HIGHER

Today's declaration is dedicated to the greatness of our God who cares for every detail (Psalm 37:23). There is none like You, O Lord; You are great, and mighty is Your name. "To Him who alone does great wonders, for His loving kindness is everlasting" (Psalm 136:4 NAS).

We stand in agreement with the Word, declaring, for as high as the heavens are above the earth, so are Your ways higher than our ways and Your thoughts than our thoughts (Isaiah 55:9). We thank You, mighty one, for You have done great things for us and holy is Your name (Luke 1:49).

Now, to You, God, who is able to do far more abundantly beyond all that we ask or think, according to the power that works within us, You have begun to show Your servants Your greatness and Your strong hand; for what god is there in heaven or on earth who can do such works and mighty acts as You do? Lord, no one can compare with You. You have done many miracles, and You plan to do many more for us. There are too many of them for us to talk about (Psalm 40:5).

Let everything (and everyone) that has breath praise the Lord (Psalm 150:6). And the word of our testimony will be on our lips today, God, for we will give thanks to You, Lord, with all our hearts, and we will tell of all Your wonderful deeds (Psalm 9:1).

In the miracle-working, way-making, mountain-moving, majestic name of King Jesus!

PRAYER:

PRAISES:

DECREE FIVE
THE LORD IS YOUR KEEPER

We confess with our mouths we know where our help comes from. Our help comes from the Lord, maker of heaven and earth. _____, the Lord is your keeper, the Lord will keep you from all evil, and He will keep your life. The Lord will keep your going out and your coming in from this time forth and forevermore (Psalm 121).

Your creator has formed you from dust, and His breath has breathed into your nostrils the breath of life, and you have become a living being. Crafted and created beautifully by the very hands of your Father in heaven. We declare over you today, as your lungs are becoming strong, the Spirit of God has made you, and the breath of the Almighty gives you life (Job 33:4).

Father, when You send forth Your Spirit, they are created. May Your glory endure forever; may You rejoice in Your works of creating, forming, sustaining, and developing _____. (Psalm 104)

We declare that as their soul prospers so will their spirit. We call forth the living Spirit of God to fill _____ with the very fruit of the Spirit being developed and deposited along with all they need in the natural in Jesus' name! We declare _____ will live and move in great measures of love, joy, peace, patience, kindness, goodness, faithfulness, gentleness, and self-control in Jesus' name.

PRAYER:

PRAISES:

DECREE SIX
KINGDOM COME

Father, today, we thank You for the gift of _____ as a gift directly from You (Psalm 127:3). You said, "Let the little children come to me, do not hinder them, for the kingdom of heaven belongs to such as these" (Matthew 19:14). So we lift up _____ to You and declare we shall see the kingdom of God manifest here on earth through the life of _____. We shall see Your mighty hand releasing heaven to _____.

Today, we bless their family with the words of God that say, "I have no greater joy than to hear that my children are walking in the truth" (3 John 1:4). Thank you, God, for their faith in holding, standing on, and believing Your truth for their lives and the life of their family member and friend.

God, we declare our confidence is in You and Your faithfulness that the good work You began in _____ You will carry it on to completion in Christ Jesus (Philippians 1:6). Father, just as Jairus (Mark 5) cried out for You to come and to lay Your hands on his daughter so that she may be made well and live, we cry out asking You to do it again!

Heal and make well this loved one. We declare by the power of Your Spirit we will walk in the obedience of Your declaration to not fear but only believe. Increase our faith to ask for, believe in, and rest in unshakable faith. To You be all glory and honor and power in Christ Jesus.

PRAYER:

PRAISES:

DECREE SEVEN
YOUR WORD

Father God, we declare today that signs, miracles, and wonders will follow those who believe You, so that all may know there is no God but You. You are the I Am, and there is no other king but Jesus (Isaiah 45:6).

Father, we praise You for this opportunity to grow in the grace and knowledge of knowing who You are (2 Peter 3:18). We stand in faith believing Your Word. You sent forth Your Word and healed them and delivered them from destruction (Psalm 107:20).

We agree and declare Your Word is alive and active, sharper than any double-edged sword or words from man. It penetrates even to dividing soul and spirit, joints and marrow. Your Word judges the thoughts and attitudes of the heart. So we ask, Lord, send forth Your Word to root out any unbelief, fear, or opinions that do not wholeheartedly believe You.

Thank you for sending Your Word to _____, so it can bring healing to every part of their being. Your Word has formed and shaped them in their mother's womb, and they are fearfully and wonderfully made in the image of God.

Father, thank You for the circumstances that allow us to know You, to know the power of Your resurrection, and for the opportunity to participate in Your sufferings so that we may become like You (Philippians 3:10-11).

By faith, we declare it pure joy, whenever we face trials of many kinds, because we know the testing of our faith produces perseverance (James 1:2-3).

In Jesus, we declare the God of all hope is filling us with joy and peace as we trust in Him for the good report of _____, and we are going to overflow with hope by the power of the Holy Spirit (Romans 15:13).

Father, we also rejoice in the love You are sending from Your people, the Body of Christ, who is standing, believing, and hoping with us. Thank you for the encouragement they have been. They have brought refreshing to the hearts of our families. We decree the blessing of God to be poured back on their own lives in great measure for their faithfulness to pray and partner with our family in Jesus' name, amen.

PRAYER:

PRAISES:

DECREE EIGHT
BE GRACIOUS

We declare God is worthy! Worthy to be loved, worthy to be pursued, worthy to be believed, and worthy to follow. In Jesus' name, we put our hope and trust in Him as our refuge and fortress.

We lift up _____, declaring You are Lord of their life, and You are their healer. We ask for both mercy and healing power over their entire body. We stand on the blood and words of Jesus declaring by His stripes you are healed, _____. You will continue to thrive and grow and heal. We continue to confess our help comes from the Lord.

Father, we declare we will not be afraid, for You are with us; we will not be dismayed, for You are our God. You will strengthen us and help us; You will uphold us with your righteous right hand (Isaiah 41:10). We lift Your Word and decree You will continue to restore health and wholeness to _____, and You will heal in Jesus' name (Jeremiah 30:17).

Lord, we ask that You would be gracious to everyone this affects. Be their strength every morning and their salvation in distress (Isaiah 33:2). God, You said that You would give strength to the weary and You would increase power of the weak (Isaiah 40:29). We humbly come in our weakness today and say, "Jesus, our Savior, we need salvation today."

We decree the Word of the Lord saying, You, the Lord are our Shepherd, we lack nothing. You make us lie down in green pastures; You lead us beside quiet waters; You refresh our soul. You are guiding us along the right paths for Your name's sake. Even though we walk through the darkest valley, we will fear no evil for You are with us. Your rod and staff comfort us. You have prepared a table for us in the presence of our enemies. You anoint our heads with oil, our cup overflows. We declare Your goodness and love will follow us all the days of our lives for we will dwell in Your house forever (Psalm 23).

God, You are our strength and portion forever. We stretch out our hand over _____, to speak healing and to perform signs and wonders through the name of Jesus (Acts 4:30-31). Fill them with Your Spirit to speak Your Word boldly. We declare we are still expecting and believing for Your miraculous hand to raise _____ to full life in Jesus' name.

PRAYER:

PRAISES:

DECREE NINE
STAND

When you have done all to stand, stand!

All praise and all glory to Jesus our sustainer and lifter of our head. Lord, we behold Your glory today and are filled with Your grace and truth (John 1:14). We declare today that light shall shine forth from darkness, and we shall walk in the knowledge of the glory of God as we see Your face (2 Corinthians 4:6).

We declare, arise _____, bless the Lord your God forever and ever. O Lord, may Your glorious name be blessed and exalted above all blessing and praise (Nehemiah 9:5). God, we pause and lift our hearts and minds to You for the glorious splendor of Your majesty, and we meditate on Your works (Psalm 145:5).

There is no one like You, Jesus, in Your majestic holiness. Awesome are Your works in Your dealings with Your children. You are working wonders in our midst (Exodus 15:11).

Thank You, God, for holding, shaping, forming, and glorifying _____'s body to wholeness and complete healing in Jesus' name. Thank you, God, for captivating and comforting this family and sustaining them by Your mighty, outstretched hands. Father, we decree that they arise and shine, for the light of Jesus has come. And the glory of the Lord has risen upon you, and His glory will appear in you, _____ (Isaiah 60:1-2).

God, You said the prayers offered in faith will make the sick person well; the Lord will raise them up. We are asking in faith for You to stretch out Your hand to heal and raise up _____ for the glory of Your name (James 5:14-15).

PRAYER:

_____

_____

_____

PRAISES:

_____

_____

_____

DECREE TEN
REST IN HIS SHADOW

Father, You said, "Whoever dwells in the shelter of the Most High will rest in the shadow of the Almighty." Thank You for the rest You are giving to each of us. Rest that is bringing refreshment, healing, and comfort to all parts of the body. Lord, You said, "When we say of the Lord, He is my refuge and my fortress, my God, in whom I trust, You, Yourself, will be our strong tower and salvation.

We declare and receive the confidence that You will cover _____ with Your feathers, and under Your wings they will find refuge; Your faithfulness will be their shield and rampart (Psalm 91). Father, we believe Your presence is covering _____ with divine protection and security in You.

Thank You that You are present in that room with them. Your Spirit is hovering and brooding as You overshadow them with

Your wings. We declare abundant, powerful, thriving life to their entire being in Jesus' name.

We declare today that we truly believe the Almighty is the Almighty!

You, God, are greater than any plan or purpose or limitation of man or science. You alone create life, and in You, _____ moves and lives and has their being (Acts 17:28).

We bless You, Lord, for creating _____. You are at work fashioning and forming them into Your mouthpiece. Thank You for the testimony of their life. Thank You for every way they will proclaim Your greatness. Thank You that You are filling their lungs and breath with Your very Word and strengthening them to speak and proclaim praises to You.

Thank you, God, for giving them a strong heart that beats in radical love, healthy kidneys that will help filter out toxins and impurities as they are growing into a lover of righteousness and purity of a life lived for Jesus. Thank you that You are giving them a sound mind that thinks and believes like Christ and will be filled with the knowledge and wisdom of You.

Father, we decree and declare today that nothing is impossible for You. We declare healing over _____'s body, guard and keep them, fill _____ with peace and strength. Protect _____'s healing process and keep them moving from strength to strength in Jesus' name.

PRAYER:

PRAISES:

DECREE ELEVEN
CADENCE OF HEAVEN TOUCHING EARTH

Father, today we declare the release of the rhythm of heaven touching earth through the partnership of man's cries interceding with the intercession of Jesus at Your right hand on behalf of _____.

Father, we continue to stand on the truth that Your ways are higher than our ways. You said that if we live by the Spirit, let us also keep in step with the Spirit (Galatians 5:25). We decree and declare _____ has been fashioned and formed in Your spirit, therefore we command all their physical systems to fall into step with the perfect rhythm and cadence of heaven for their health and healing in Jesus' name.

We ask right now that as You, God, sing songs of rejoicing over _____ that they rest in Your delight over them, knowing their God is with them, the mighty warrior who saves (Zephaniah 3:17). God, we declare Your words with confidence, because they love You. You will rescue them; You will protect them for they acknowledge Your name.

We are acknowledging You, Jesus! Jesus! Jesus! You alone are the way, the truth, and the life.

We will call on You, and You will answer us; You are with us in trouble, and You will deliver and honor. With long life You will satisfy _____ and show them Your salvation (Psalm 91).

God, we confess You are enough for _____. You are all and everything they need. Sweep them up in Your arms of healing and rock their body to the cadence and rhythm of love that brings strength and wholeness to their spirit, body, and soul.

Father, give us grace today to know Your ways that we may know You. We cry out for Your glory to be revealed so all shall see it (Isaiah 40:5).

God, we trust that You have gone before us and are in front of _____ in every step, and You have proclaimed, "The Lord God is compassionate and gracious, slow to anger, and abounding in lovingkindness and truth" (Exodus 34:6). Today, we rest in Your abounding loving kindness. You alone are our hope and peace.

PRAYER:

PRAISES:

DECREE TWELVE
SIGNIFICANCE OF NUMBERS

As I began to write the twelfth decree, I couldn't help but notice the significance of that number. For example, Jesus healed a woman who had been bleeding for twelve years, twelve tribes of Judah, twelve disciples, twelve stones embedded in the high priest's breastplate, twelve baskets of bread leftover, and these are just a few examples of the significance of the number twelve in the Scripture. Twelve in Scripture often relates to divine government, God's authority, perfection, and completeness.

So today's declaration will be tied to the fact that there are no accidents in the kingdom of God. And since this is the twelfth declaration, I am relying on the authority of God, who rules and reigns over all things in perfection and completeness, to declare that we agree with Him here on earth for everything that touches heaven. Our intercession desires to be full of the very prayers Jesus is interceding on behalf of our loved one at the right hand of God.

Father, we declare today that You reign above it all! Above every concern, every need, every question, and every circumstance _____ may find themselves in. You are over it all, and in Your perfection, You are working all things for their good. For by You, God, all things were created, both in heaven and on earth, visible and invisible, whether thrones or dominions or rulers or authorities—all things have been created through You and for You (Colossians 1:16).

We declare, You have authority over _____'s body, and all parts of their body are subject to Your authority and completion. For we are confident of this very thing, You, God, began a good work in _____, and You are perfecting it in Christ Jesus (Philippians 1:6).

In Christ, _____ has been made complete, lacking nothing for Christ is the head, the ruler and authority over your being (Colossians 2:10). Therefore, we speak to every vital system in your body, and we, by the authority of Jesus, speak healing, wholeness, and thriving life to your heart, lungs, kidneys, and brain.

We declare, God, we will not become weary in doing good. We will fight as good soldiers, allowing endurance to have its perfect result, so that _____ may be perfect and complete, lacking in nothing, for we trust our good Father, who supplies all good and perfect things (James 1:4).

Thank You for continued wisdom and favor being poured out over this family in Your sight and man's. We trust You as their complete provision. Thank You, God, for supplying every need abundantly. _____, God is able to bless you abundantly, so that in all things, at all times, having all that you need, you will abound in every good work (2 Corinthians 9:8).

We declare today, _____, that out of God's glorious riches He will strengthen you with power through His Spirit in your inner being (Ephesians 3:16).

PRAYER:

_____

_____

_____

_____

_____

_____

_____

_____

_____

PRAISES:

DECREE THIRTEEN
ALL HOPE

Father, we declare, You are the God who holds it all. By faith, we understand that the universe was created by Your words, so that what is seen was not made out of things that are visible (Hebrews 11:3). We believe You are the same yesterday, today, and forever and by faith, believe You are using Your Word to fashion and form _____ from all that is unseen.

Today, we proclaim we can trust You. We can trust Your working. We can trust Your healing. We can trust Your providing. And mostly, we can trust You are present—Emmanuel, God with us and with _____.

In Your presence is fullness. Thank you for creating _____ in Your fullness. Father, today we decree as we stand and wait upon You. By faith, we believe You will not delay, and we will not shrink back in contending for healing and wholeness for

_____, for we are those who have faith (Hebrews 10:39).

God, today, with praise on our lips to You, the One who is worthy, and with thanksgiving in our hearts, we bless Your holy name. By faith, against all hope, we hope in You, for You are the God of all hope. We decree that hope arise!

We proclaim that against any odds that come against _____ in any way, we will not relent, and we will not be moved. We will stand our ground and hold our position to accomplish the purposes and destiny of _____, according to Your will for their life and their position as Your child.

_____, as part of your spiritual inheritance, I call your spirit to attention in the name of Jesus. _____, I call your whole being into Christ-likeness. I speak to your heart and declare your heart beats to the rhythm, determination, and strength of the powerful love of God. I speak to your mind and decree God is transforming your mind to the very mind of Christ, nothing lacking, full of the glory of God!

I speak healing to your mind and release the power of God to make perfect all in and out flow of blood to it. I speak to your lungs that they would move and function on the very wind of heaven, the breath of God sustaining and strengthening their function apart from man's intervention.

Holy Spirit is your respirator, regulating your inhaling and exhaling in perfect alignment. I speak to your kidneys and declare continued filtering in rhythmic partnership with the rest of your body, according to kingdom design, which brings health to your body.

_____, I speak to your spirit, created and designed by your Father in heaven, and declare it is strong; it is feisty. You have the tenacity of a bulldog, the fearlessness of a lion, the sight and hearing of an eagle, and your inner being like an owl that cooperates with the wisdom of God.

_____, you are a beloved, strong, and adored child of God, born for such a time as this to reveal the majesty and mighty hand of our God. To Him be all glory and honor for speaking you into being. We will forever praise His name, for He is good and what He does is good.

PRAYER:

PRAISES:

DECREE FOURTEEN
BLOOD OF THE LAMB

Father, today we come giving thanks for the saints who are interceding and storming the gates of heaven on _____'s behalf. Thank You for their prayers, thank You for their perseverance, thank You for commitment and willingness to interrupt their lives to petition You on our behalf. We are forever grateful.

We declare Your Word that says, if any two on earth agree about what they ask for, it will be done for them by our Father in heaven (Matthew 18:19). We come into agreement for the life of _____ and ask You to heal and grow their body into completion in Jesus' name.

We will proclaim to all who witness this miracle it is only by the name of Jesus that _____ stands before us healed and whole (Acts 4:10). We stand by faith in the name of Jesus, declaring this person whom you see and know has been made strong. It is Jesus' name and the faith that comes through Him that has completely healed them for all to see (Acts 3:16).

_____, you will proclaim the praises and glory of the hand of your God!

God, we declare, we may be hard pressed on every side, but we are not crushed; we may be perplexed but not in despair; persecuted, but never abandoned; struck down, but we shout we will not be destroyed (2 Corinthians 4:8-10).

We will be those who rejoice in the Lord always (Philippians 4:4). Father, You give the example in Acts 4 where Peter, John, and the people stood in agreement and prayed, "enable us to stretch out our hands to heal and perform signs and wonders through the name of your holy servant Jesus." We stand asking You, God, do it again. Stretch out Your hand over _____ and perform miracles in Jesus' name.

After they were done praying, the place where they prayed was shaken, and they were filled with the Holy Spirit. Fill _____ with Your Spirit that shakes things into right kingdom order. Let the fire of Your Spirit fall in that room, touching not only _____ but all others who are sick and needing healing in there. Heal them all, Lord.

Father, we proclaim that Your wisdom and understanding fill this room and all those who enter this atmosphere be filled with increased discernment, wisdom, and compassion for the precise care _____ needs to thrive. When adjusting medications and machines, they do so with precision and with the utmost benefit for _____'s healing process in Jesus' name.

In the name of Jesus, _____, you will arise and be healed.

Father, we declare stability and regulation to their blood pressure and command it to stay in the range that benefits their healing process. Lord, we speak a good report to any and all future testing on _____'s progress in Jesus' name.

Lord, we exalt You in all ways. For Your name's sake, continue to lead, guide, direct, and show all who are connected to _____ Your ways.

Father, in the authority of Jesus, we stand in the gap, repent, and declare if there be any known or unknown generational iniquities in this family line, they are forgiven. In the righteousness of Christ, we take back all health the enemy has tried to steal from this generational line, and we speak divine health to be replaced in _____.

_____, you have been redeemed by the blood of the Lamb from every curse of the law of sin, sickness, infirmity, or disease. We command any further effects of weakness and sickness to leave your body, and we decree the release of God's creative miracle-working power to enter your body, to heal, restore, deliver, and make whole in the majestic name of Jesus.

Today, we decree is a major turnaround day. Jehovah Raphe is your healer. _____, your being submits to your Creator. Thank You, Lord, for hearing and moving upon our prayers. We ask for reinforcement angels to come to their aid, to nurture, protect, and fulfill Your every word, God. _____, we decree You are a beloved child of God.

PRAYER:

PRAISES:

DECREE FIFTEEN
HE HEARS US

Father, we declare that we will rejoice always, pray without ceasing, as we give thanks in all circumstances; for this is Your will in Christ Jesus (1 Thessalonians 5:16-17).

We proclaim our confidence and gratitude in approaching such a holy and powerful God, who has given us permission and authority to ask anything, according to His will, and He hears us (1 John 5:14). Our hearts are full to overflowing in the truth that our God hears our prayers. And if we know He hears us, whatever we ask, we can then know we have what we asked of Him (1 John 5:15).

Thank you, Lord, for so many answers to prayer.

We will declare the mighty working power of our God. We will continually look to the Lord and His strength concerning _____ and will seek His face always (1 Chronicles 16:11).

God, we declare our desire is to have the eyes of our hearts opened and enlightened in order that we may know the hope to which You have called us and the riches of Your glorious inheritance (Ephesians 1:18).

_____, we declare the petition to God for your inheritance of good health and long life in Christ, with the assurance that God hears and answers our prayers. _____, as we pray in the Spirit, on your behalf, on all occasions, with all kinds of prayers and requests, we remain on alert and declare we will keep on praying for all the Lord has designed and purposed for you (Ephesians 6:18).

God, over and over in Your Word, You command Your people to pray with the promise that You will listen, hear, and fulfill. Thank You for Your promise to answer our cries on behalf of _____. Thank You for the miraculous answers thus far; we declare we will not stop.

Father, increase our faith to believe that once we have asked, we will receive and what we have asked in Jesus' name will be ours (Mark 11:24). God, we call on You today to work mighty miracles in _____'s entire body, restoring lungs, kidneys, heart, and brain to full capacity, with no weakness, lack, or struggle in Jesus' name.

In their weakness, God, Your strength is made completely perfect. Thank You for perfecting them. Thank You that You have put the heart of a feisty, persistent, bold warrior in _____. Thank You that the spirit of love, joy, and peace is their covering and protection in Jesus' name.

Thank You that Your hand is protecting and keeping them from retaining any and all trauma from medical procedures, as we are trusting You to rewrite all memories of trauma in Your love and joy. No trauma, fear, or grief gets to remain. We declare _____ is shrouded in Your glory, and in You there is no darkness or trauma.

We ask for the fire of Your Spirit to fill this room as You continue to provide exactly what _____ needs in every manner for abundant life, growth, and health as they live for Your glory. Thank You for Your continued care and provision and healing.

PRAYER:

PRAISES:

DECREE SIXTEEN
NO GREATER LOVE

We declare the Word of God that there is no greater love than a man lay down His life for his friend (John 15:13). Jesus, we celebrate the power of Your love laid down that we may have life.

_____, we declare that you shall know the love of God for you, for He showed you His love by sending His one and only Son into the world that you would live through Him. This is love, not that we loved God first but that He loves you, _____, and sent His Son as a sacrifice for you (1 John 4:9-11).

And so, we know and rely on the love God has for us (1 John 4:16). _____, we are depending on the powerful love of God that saves to heal, restore, strengthen, and keep you in perfect peace because He loves you.

We declare it is the love of God that allows us to proclaim that in all things we are more than conquerors.

_____, you are a mighty conqueror through Him who loves you (Romans 8:37). There is no mountain or obstacle you face that can keep you from the unshakable and unfailing covenant of love and peace God has for you (Isaiah 54:10).

We receive God's great love for you and declare His love is making you rich in mercy and alive in Christ, for it is by His grace He is saving you (Ephesians 2:4-5). Today, we give thanks to God in heaven, for His love endures forever (Psalm 136:26).

Thank you, God, that your love never leaves _____. You are present with them always, and the love of their mighty warrior is saving them, for You take great delight in showing Your powerful love to _____ (Zephaniah 3:17).

We unashamedly ask You to pour out lavish love on _____ that the world would know Your love. Father, we decree we will not become weary in doing good, for in Your proper time we will reap the harvest of every word You have spoken about and to _____. We will not give up (Galatians 6:9).

We celebrate the peace and miracles You are performing in _____'s body and spirit. We are joyful in hope, patient in our affliction, and faithful in prayer (Romans 12:12). We present our requests to You today, God. Continue to heal, grow, and strengthen this courageous, mighty warrior. Strengthen them by the power of Your Spirit in boldness and courage. Increase the presence of Your Spirit moving through every vein in their body, giving life and wholeness to all organs and tissues and muscles in Jesus' name!

God, You said a day is as a thousand years to You, and a thousand years is as a day. You are not bound to time as we are, so we ask today, in Your grace, expedite man's timetable and heal _____ quickly, supernaturally.

We decree over you, _____, that you are not bound by weeks and what man thinks you are capable of according to earth's time. You defy the limitations of earth because your home is in the kingdom of God, and He is bringing His kingdom into your body. Be free to grow, move, and heal according to God's plan, not man's, in Jesus' name.

PRAYER:

PRAISES:

DECREE SEVENTEEN
NO GOD, BUT JESUS!

We praise You, God. You alone are worthy to be praised. God, today seems like a fiery furnace day, and like Shadrach, Meshach, and Abednego, we answer the fire declaring, "if you throw us into the hot furnace, the God we serve can save us… but even if He does not, we will not serve any God but Jesus" (Daniel 3).

Father, we know life can turn up the heat that feels hotter than usual, and it can feel like we are tied up tighter than we can escape from, but we declare there is another Man in the fire with us!

By faith, we declare the fire will not destroy us, but rather, we will come out of the fire praising, for You are sending forth Your angels to save Your servants from the fire. Our trust is in You, God, and we refuse to obey doubt, fear, or intimidation around these circumstances. We will serve and worship only You, God.

God, You spoke _____ into existence for this moment in time. You have divine purpose and intent for their every breath. We are contending, God, for the miracle of life. Bring healing to every part of their being. Strengthen, restore, and bring to kingdom order all systems in Jesus' name.

We ask for continued divine protection over _____ and their family. Protect their hearts, minds, and faith in Jesus' name. Make them as strong as mountains that cannot be shaken. We declare we are firm in faith, for You are mighty to deliver. Father, we ask for miraculous reports today concerning _____. Guard their mind, heart, kidneys, and lungs, giving supernatural power to heal, strengthen, and restore in the mighty name that has authority over all things.

Give kingdom wisdom and strategies for excellent care to every doctor and nurse in Jesus' name. _____, we declare you are fearfully and wonderfully made. You are a force of God to be reckoned with. You have the Spirit of God in you, and you shall live and move at His command. We speak to your spirit and say, arise and shine, for the light of Jesus is upon you.

PRAYER:

PRAISES:

DECREE EIGHTEEN
MIGHTY TO SAVE

Father, we declare that You are mighty to save and full of mercy. We declare Your mercy over _____. Deal with them according to Your steadfast love and according to Your abundant mercy (Psalm 51:1). Father, we praise You for the blessing that _____ is.

We stand on Your Word declaring, "Yet this I call to mind and therefore I have hope: because of the Lord's great love we are not consumed, for his compassions never fail. They are new every morning; great is your faithfulness. I say to myself, 'The Lord is my portion; therefore I will wait for him.' The Lord is good to those whose hope is in him, to the one who seeks him; it is good to wait quietly for the salvation of the Lord" (Lamentations 3:21-26).

As we wait on You, Lord, we declare we do so in hope. For You are a merciful God, and our trust is in You alone. Today, we draw near with a true heart in full assurance of faith, holding fast to the confession of our hope, without wavering for You who promised is faithful concerning _____ (Hebrews 10:23).

We praise You for the life of _____. Thank You for sustaining and keeping them in the palm of Your hand. We contend for complete and total healing. Thank You for every good and stable moment. Give their family sustaining rest and wisdom. Carry them close to Your heart as You meet them in their every need. We glorify Your name—our miracle-working God!

PRAYER:

PRAISES:

DECREE NINETEEN
PEACEFUL HABITATION

Father, today we stand in faith, choosing to believe You are working miracles on _____'s behalf. Thank you, Lord, for being their comforter, sustainer, and healer. Thank You for every breath, movement, and heartbeat. We thank You for providing a sound mind for them. Thank You for regulating their lungs and filtering the air they breath. Thank You that You are revealing Your glory in and through _____'s life.

We declare, _____, you belong to God, and you will abide in peaceful habitation in a secure dwelling and in a quiet resting place (Isaiah 32:18).

Thank You, Lord, that _____'s room is a place of miracles where Your Spirit and presence dwell with them in constant communion. Thank You for ministering and delighting in _____ as You remain present to heal their mind, body, and soul. Thank You, God, for bringing stabilization to their body and all functions and systems in Jesus' name.

We ask today for an increase of Your grace in the waiting as You incubate this miracle. We declare that we will not be afraid or discouraged, for You will personally go ahead of us. You will be with _____ and neither fail nor abandon them (Deuteronomy 31:8).

We proclaim You, Lord, are a shield about _____. You are their glory and the lifter of their head. We speak a lifting to happen today—a lifting of spirits, health, energy, and strength in Jesus' name. We ask that Your power infuse joy, strength, and might to their body in Jesus' name!

Thank You, Lord, that You are answering from your holy mountain (Psalm 3:3-4). Father, we ask for an infusion of peace to fill _____'s body that comes from You. We decree our hearts will not be troubled or filled with fears, for our hope and peace comes in abundant supply from You alone (John 14:27).

_____, we speak to your spirit and body and declare this is a good day, a day to rejoice in the Lord. We celebrate you and every victory toward your healing. You are cherished and loved with a perfect love of a good Father.

_____, Jesus is watching over you; He is molding and shaping you in His image. You are safe, protected, and cared for. In rest, you will find healing, and in peace, you will be restored.

PRAYER:

_____

_____

_____

_____

_____

PRAISES:

_____

_____

_____

_____

_____

DECREE TWENTY
PERFECT PEACE

Lord, we celebrate every day of life You have given _____. You are faithful. We decree that You are keeping in perfect peace those who trust in You and have fixed their thoughts on You (Isaiah 26:3). We continue to declare You, God, are our source of hope and You are filling _____ completely to overflowing measure with joy and peace because they trust in You.

Because of Your filling, they will overflow with confident hope through the power of Holy Spirit (Romans 15:13). Father, You said that without faith it is impossible to please You. Thank You for faith. We decree Your promise to reward those who earnestly seek You (Hebrews 11:6).

We thank You, Lord, for teaching us to live by faith and not by sight (2 Corinthians 5:7). We praise You for Your graciousness toward us as we have cried out to You for help. As soon as You have heard our prayers, You answer (Isaiah 30:19). God, You said to bring our petitions to You, ask in Your name, and You would do it for Your Son to bring glory to You.

We are asking You to heal, strengthen, and mature _____ to bring You glory (John 14:13-14). Our Father in heaven, Your name is holy. May Your kingdom come into this room, into _____'s body, and may Your will be done in them as it is in heaven. Today, give all that they need to prosper in body and soul for abundant life in Jesus' name (Matthew 6:9-13).

We decree today, _____, you shall thrive, rest, live, and grow to the glory of God. You shall have no weakness, limitation, or lack, for your Father in heaven is supplying all your needs according to the riches He has stored up for you in heaven. We give God all honor and all glory.

PRAYER:

PRAISES:

DECREE TWENTY-ONE
FOUND FAITHFUL

Today, we declare the greatness of You, creator God. Thank You for creating _____. We decree we do not grieve or face trials as the world does, for You are the God of all hope; therefore, we hope. We declare, by Your grace, we shall not worry about anything. Instead, we will be found faithful to pray about all things.

We will tell God what we need and thank Him for all He has done (Philippians 4:6).

Thank You, Lord, for Your steadfast love that never ceases and Your mercies that never end. They are new every morning, for great is Your faithfulness. We praise You for Your faithfulness in showing _____ Your new mercies every morning (Lamentations 3:22-23).

We declare our praise to You who is able to do immeasurably more than all we ask or imagine, according to Your power at work within _____ (Ephesians 3:20).

Father, we declare over _____, be strong and let your heart take courage as we wait together for the Lord (Psalm 31:24). As we wait upon the Lord to work abundant miracles in _____, we shout our God is good!

PRAYER:

PRAISES:

DECREE TWENTY-TWO
WITH US

We are confident in this, neither death nor life, nor angels nor rulers, nor things present nor things to come, nor powers, nor height nor depth, nor anything else in all creation will be able to separate us from the love of God in Christ Jesus our Lord (Romans 8:38-39).

Thank You, Lord, for Your constant companionship with _____. Thank You for being with them at every milestone. Thank You for allowing nothing to separate them from Your presence and Your love for them. Thank You for loving this family in the midst of all that is going on. Thank You that there is nothing that can come between You and Your love for them.

We declare today, God, You are good, and You do good things. Teach us Your ways (Psalm 119:68). Lord, You are good to all, and Your mercies are all over _____.

Thank You for protecting, providing, and preparing _____ for their life of glorifying You (Psalm 145:9).

God, we declare Your Word that says, You have done all things well; You make even the deaf to hear and the blind to see. Developing, progressing, and healing _____ is no challenge for You. We declare You have made _____ well (Mark 7:37). We praise You, God.

_____, we declare that your life will radiate the goodness of our God. Your health and wholeness, _____, will proclaim, "Come and see the works of God, who is awesome in His deeds toward the sons of men" (Psalm 66:5 NAS).

PRAYER:

_____

_____

_____

_____

_____

_____

_____

PRAISES:

DECREE TWENTY-THREE
PRAISEWORTHY

"Whatever things are true, whatever things are noble, whatever things are just, whatever things are pure, whatever things are lovely, whatever things are of good report, if there is any virtue and if there is anything praiseworthy—meditate on these things" (Philippians 4:8 NKJV).

Lord, we declare we will meditate and think on every good and perfect thing that comes from Your hand. Thank You, that You have made _____, pure and lovely. You are doing noble and just things in their life, and You are bringing about good reports. We praise You for we know You are their great physician, You are their healer. We declare You are worthy of all praise.

"Then shall your light break forth like the dawn, and your healing shall spring up speedily; your righteousness shall go before you; the glory of the Lord shall be your rear guard" (Isaiah 58:8 ESV).

We praise You, God, that the light of Jesus is breaking forth in healing and wholeness in and over _____ and their healing shall spring up speedily.

Thank You that the glory of the Lord covers _____ and is keeping them free from all infections. We declare that _____ is the beloved of the Lord. Therefore, we pray that all may go well with them and they may be in good health, as it goes well with their soul (3 John 1:2).

_____, we decree because you not only grow in physical health and wholeness and healing, but you will also grow in the fear of the Lord and in His name. The sun of righteousness shall rise with healing in its wings. You shall go out leaping like calves from the stall (Malachi 4:2).

We speak that the miracle-working power of the resurrected Christ is making your skin perfect as silken and tawny as a field of wheat touched by the breeze (Song of Songs 7:2). Hear your Father declare over you, _____, you are altogether beautiful, my darling. There is no flaw in you (Song of Songs 4:7).

Thank you, God, for healing them flawlessly, and thank You they shall lack no good thing. Father, we praise You for those caring for and working on _____'s behalf. Give them rest, wisdom beyond their understanding, and compassion that comes from You, the God of compassion.

Continue to bless and release divine wisdom and victorious strategies to the doctors and nurses.

PRAYER:

PRAISES:

DECREE TWENTY-FOUR
STEADFAST NOT SHAKEN

We declare:

"Praise the Lord. Blessed are those who fear the Lord, who find great delight in his commands. Their children will be mighty in the land; the generation of the upright will be blessed. Wealth and riches are in their houses, and their righteousness endures forever. Even in darkness light dawns for the upright, for those who are gracious and compassionate and righteous. Good will come to those who are generous and lend freely, who conduct their affairs with justice.

Surely the righteous will never be shaken; they will be remembered forever. They will have no fear of bad news; their hearts are steadfast, trusting in the Lord. Their hearts are secure, they will have no fear; in the end they will look in triumph on their foes. They have freely scattered their gifts to the poor, their righteousness endures forever; their horn will be lifted high in honor. The wicked will see and be vexed, they will gnash their teeth and waste away; the longings of the wicked will come to nothing" (Psalm 112:1-10).

Father, we decree we stand firmly on Your Word and will not be shaken! We will not fear any report of man but hold tightly to Your report concerning _____'s life.

You said _____ will be mighty in the land, and they will be blessed. We decree _____'s heart is secure, and they shall have no fear. We decree we are steadfastly trusting in You for working out _____'s healing and restoration.

We declare no weapon or scheme that the enemy forms against _____ will have any chance of prospering in Jesus' name. Every bad report or tongue that tries to rise against _____ in pronouncing judgment, God will Himself condemn. _____, you shall believe only the report of the Lord for your life. This is your inheritance in the Lord. Jesus is your righteousness (Isaiah 54:17).

Lord, You said the righteous cry out, and You hear them; You will deliver them from all their troubles. We are standing on Your very Word. You said if we cried out, You would heal all _____'s troubles—not one left unhealed.

You said ALL! Anything we have not proclaimed healing over, show us we can cry out for it.

We decree every system, function, flow, intake, and output be in line with the kingdom of God. We speak the peace of God is filling and flooding _____'s body, bringing health, wholeness, and rest that heals in Jesus' name. We will see the miracle-working hand of God in _____'s life in Jesus' name.

PRAYER:

PRAISES:

DECREE TWENTY-FIVE
HEALING WINGS

_____, you are one who dwells in the shelter of the Most High; therefore, you will abide in the shadow of the Almighty. You will say to the Lord, my refuge and my fortress, my God in whom I trust. For God will deliver you from the snare of the fowler and from the deadly disease. Your God will cover you with His pinions, and under His healing wings you will find refuge; His faithfulness is a shield about you and a buckler. You shall not fear the terror of the night, nor the arrow that flies by day, nor any pestilence that stalks in darkness, nor the destruction that wastes at noonday.

A thousand may fall at your side, _____, ten thousand at your right hand, but it will not come near you. You will only look with your eyes and see the payback of the wicked. Because the Lord is your dwelling place, _____, the Most High is your refuge; no evil shall be allowed to befall you, nor any plague come near your dwelling. For God is commanding His angels concerning you to guard you in all your ways. Because we hold fast to the Lord in love, He will deliver you, _____. He will protect you because you shall know His name.

When we call to Him, He answers. God is with you now, _____, and He is rescuing you with honor. With long life God is satisfying you and showing you salvation (Psalm 91). We declare the praises of our God, for it is good to give thanks to the Lord. With all our hearts we sing praises to the name that is above all names.

Oh, Most High, we declare Your steadfast love in the morning and Your faithfulness by night (Psalm 92). Father, we praise You for the wisdom and direction You are pouring out to the physicians and nurses for _____'s care. Thank You for divine strategy from the works of Your hands, God. Thank You for loving _____ more than we ever could.

PRAYER:

_____

_____

_____

_____

_____

_____

PRAISES:

DECREE TWENTY-SIX
JUST ONE TOUCH

Father, today, we declare from the mountains and even in the valleys that You are so worthy of every ounce of praise. Thank You for stretching us and our faith, making more room for Your faithfulness and goodness in our hearts. Thank You for showing us in greater measures that we are not in control. Thank You for showing us and convincing us deep within our souls Your ways are always better. We confess our questions, our momentary doubts in an outcome, and ask You to cleanse us with Your forgiveness as we arise in unshakable faith, knowing You are always good (Psalm 13).

Thank You for the assurance that there is no doubt we can trust Your unfailing steadfast love for _____. Thank You, Lord, for showing Yourself faithful to the faithful. Therefore, we decree and declare we love You, Lord, for You are our strength. You are _____'s rock, fortress, and deliverer, and in You they have found refuge. You are their stronghold and nothing can shake them from Your hand.

We call to You, Lord, on _____'s behalf. You are so worthy of praise, and they are saved from every enemy to their well-being, wholeness, and healing because of You. From Your temple, Lord, You have heard our cries for help concerning _____. Our cries have come before You, into Your ears, and in mercy, we ask boldly for You to part the heavens and come. Your powerful voice causes our enemies to scatter. At Your command, You reach down from heaven and rescue us from our powerful enemies (Psalm 18).

Creator God, we ask You to reach down from on high and take hold of _____. One touch from You changes, renews, transforms, and heals. Draw them out of stress, draw them out of weakness, draw them out of any lack and into fullness for in Christ there is fullness and wholeness. You alone, God, are their support.

_____ we say to you, you are not dependent on those machines or medications. Your support comes from the Lord. He is bringing you into spacious places and rescuing you, for He delights in you. It is God who is arming you with strength, _____. He is making your feet like the deer, for you will stand on the heights declaring His greatness. He, Himself, is training your hands for battle, _____. Your arms will have the strength to bend bows of bronze. Gods help is your shield, and it is His right hand that sustains you. We declare it is God's help that is making you great, healthy, and whole. Today, we declare the Lord lives! Praise be to our Rock! Exalted be God our Savior! (Psalm 18).

PRAYER:

PRAISES:

DECREE TWENTY-SEVEN
WATCHMEN ON THE WALL

We come into agreement with the Word of God and proclaim with confidence, "Not one promise from God is empty of power, for nothing is impossible with God" (Luke 1:37). We decree today that every good word spoken over _____ shall come to pass.

Thank You, Lord, for speaking, declaring, and pronouncing Your Word into their very being. Thank You for infusing into their spirit Your words of life, healing, and transformation. Your Word stands as watchmen on the wall over their very life. Thank You for assigning angelic armies that move at the sound of Your Word to perform what You send forth to accomplish in _____'s body. We shout, Your Word never fails!

_____, you shall hear the Word of the Lord, and all your mind, heart, and body shall respond and obey the commands of the Lord. We rejoice in this day the Lord has made.

Jesus, You are the joy and delight of our hearts, and You are worthy of praise. We praise You for every breath _____ takes. We praise You for the blessing they are and for the works of Your hands as You, the great physician, tend to and touch them into completeness and healing.

_____, we declare over you rest in His healing, for there is healing in His rest. Day and night, _____, the Word of God leads, directs, and guides your every move, bringing you into health and wholeness. _____, you are strengthened, complete, and perfected, for God has given you everything you need in Him to prosper (Hebrews 13:21-2, 2 Timothy 3:16-17).

_____, we decree you are a gift from God. You are a reward, straight from the hand of God (Psalm 127:3). We decree the light of Jesus resides in you. We believe in the light of Jesus. He is shaping you into His light bearer, and your life will reflect the power of His light that penetrates darkness and releases the power of God to transform and heal in Jesus' name (John 12:36).

God, You said that out of the mouths of nursing babies and infants You have established strength that stills the enemies and releases praises to our King (Psalm 8:2). O Lord, how

majestic is Your name! We praise You for a peaceful night over
_____. Thank You for Your peace that rests upon them.

PRAYER:

PRAISES:

DECREE TWENTY-EIGHT
SOVEREIGN

The Mighty One, God, You have spoken and summoned the earth from the rising of the sun to its setting (Psalm 50:1). We acknowledge and decree Your authority and sovereignty over all things, Lord. We decree You are sovereign over _____. "'For I the LORD will speak, and whatever word I speak will be performed. It will no longer be delayed...I will speak the word and perform it,' declares the Lord God" (Ezekiel 12:25 NAS).

God, You said that _____ would come through the fire because You are with them in it, and Your Word says that when You're with us in the fire, we won't even smell like smoke. We are trusting Your faithfulness to perform Your Word. Thank You for no more delay. We continue to stand asking for supernatural time and that You would perform miracles quickly on their behalf.

We thank You and praise You for every miracle that You are performing in their body and on their behalf. Thank You, God, that Your Word promises You do extraordinary miracles by the hands of Your servants (Acts 19:11). We bless the hands of doctors, nurses, therapists, and anyone else who touches _____ to perform extraordinary miracles concerning them, all for Your name's sake. You are the God who works wonders. You have made known Your might among the peoples (Psalm 77:14). We praise You for a miracle turnaround in the strengthening and healing of _____.

Our prayer is that anyone working with or hearing about Your hand of miracle-working power in the life of _____ that does not know You personally would, as in Exodus 14:31, see Your great power to deliver and heal _____, and it will cause them to fear You in awe and wonder and they would believe in You and be saved. Lord, expand Your kingdom and grow Your family as You release signs, miracles, and wonders before our very eyes.

PRAYER:

_____

_____

_____

_____

PRAISES:

DECREE TWENTY-NINE
FACE OF GOD

"The Lord bless you and keep you; the Lord make his face shine on you and be gracious to you; the Lord turn his face toward you and give you peace" (Numbers 6:24-26). _____, we bless you today to look upon the face of your God. _____, as you gaze into the face of God, may your whole being be filled with the peace of God.

Father, thank You for every blessing and touch that You are pouring out that brings strength and healing to _____'s body. Pour out Your abundant grace upon every inch of _____'s body to empower them to health and wholeness in Christ.

Lord, we declare You are gracious to us and make Your face to shine upon us so that Your ways may be known on earth, Your salvation among all nations (Psalm 67:2). Let all know You are still the God who performs miracles. You are still the God who rules and reigns over death, sickness, and weakness. You are still the God who hears and moves upon the prayers of Your children. You hear our cries, and Your compassionate heart moves on our behalf. You are still the God who tramples on darkness to reveal Your kingdom here on earth.

All praises to our God, who is alive, active, and moving on behalf of _____. You alone are turning things around for their good. We decree that today is to be a banner breakthrough day in their healing process. Thank You, Father, that the banner over _____ is Your powerful and healing love for them.

PRAYER:

_____
_____
_____
_____
_____
_____
_____
_____

PRAISES:

DECREE THIRTY
REMEMBER

"I will remember the deeds of the Lord; yes, I will remember your miracles of long ago" (Psalm 77:11). We decree time and again, God, You remind us in Your Word of all the miracles You performed on behalf of Your children. Therefore, we will consider all Your works and meditate on all Your mighty deeds. Your ways, God, are holy. What god is as great as our God? You are the God who performs miracles. You display Your power among the peoples.

We declare, God, display Your power in _____. Display Your splendor as You perform mighty acts of healing on their behalf.

_____, you will remember the works of God's hand on your very life sustaining, restoring, and keeping you.

With our voice we declare that we will tell the stories of Your miracles and deliverance, "We will not hide them from our descendants; we will tell the next generation the praiseworthy deeds of the Lord, his power, and the wonders he has done" (Psalm 78:4). "So the next generation would know them, even the children yet to be born, and they in turn would tell their children. Then they would put their trust in God and would not forget his deeds but would keep his commands" (Psalm 78:6-7).

_____, you will not forget the hand of your Redeemer and healer and of His mighty acts. You will proclaim them to the next generation (Psalm 145:4).

We declare, we will not turn back on the day of battle; we will keep God's covenant and live by the commands of God. For we will remember that God is our rock and that God Most High is your Redeemer, _____ (Psalm 78).

Thank You, God, for strengthening and healing _____. We decree what man says is not possible is more than possible with You, God! Thank You for continuing to shape and mold _____ into being with Your mighty, righteous hands. Thank You for perfecting and crowning them with grace and dignity as You grow _____ in Your image.

PRAYER:

PRAISES:

DECREE THIRTY-ONE
AT THE SOUND

We ascribe to the Lord all the glory due His name; we worship the Lord in the splendor of holiness. We decree over _____, you shall hear the voice of the Lord for the voice of the Lord is over the waters. Your God of glory thunders. His voice is powerful and full of majesty. At the sound of His voice, everything else bows. The voice of the Lord flashes forth flames of fire. His voice shakes loose all that can be shaken. The Lord sits enthroned over you, _____.

He is enthroned as king forever. May the Lord give strength to your body and soul. May the Lord bless you with peace (Psalm 29). We decree blessings over your entire body as you rest in the sound of His voice. We decree no other voice will you follow, no other voice but the powerful voice of truth. What God has declared and spoken over you and to you will you respond to. The voice of God covers you as He covers the earth. His voice speaks into existence all that there is. His voice is filled with creative power. At the sound of His voice, the angels dispatch and minister everything He has spoken and decreed for your life, _____.

God says, you are His child, created in His image (John 1:12). God says, _____, Jesus is your friend who sticks closer to you than a brother (Proverbs 18:24). You have been bought with the precious blood of Jesus, and you belong to God (1 Corinthians 6:19-20). God speaks, you are complete in Christ (Colossians 2:10).

_____, the voice of God declares over you assurance that He is working all things together for your good (Romans 8:28). You are established, anointed, and sealed by God (2 Corinthians 1:21-22).

We praise You, God, that You have hidden _____ in You. They are safe, secure, and covered by love. God, You spoke Your Word, and we can be confident that the good work You began in _____ will be perfected (Philippians 1:6).

_____, we decree you have been chosen and appointed to bear much fruit (John 15:16).

PRAYER:

PRAISES:

DECREE THIRTY-TWO
CALL YOU BLESSED

Father, as I read in Luke today, I sense you highlighting Luke 1:46 over _____. _____, we declare that your soul will magnify the Lord, and your spirit rejoices in God your Savior, for He has looked on the humble state of your being. Behold, _____, from now on all generations will call you blessed; for HE who is mighty has done great things for you, and holy is His name.

_____, it is by the hand of God, who is your Savior, that many will come to know Him through His work in your life. Today, we decree the prayer Jesus taught to His disciples: Father, hallowed be Your name. Your kingdom come, Your will be done in _____ on earth as it is in heaven. Give them this day their daily bread (Matthew 6:9, 12).

All that they need to thrive today comes from Your hand, God.

Forgive us all of our sins, for we forgive everyone who is indebted to us. And lead us not into temptation, guard our hearts and minds from all fear, doubt, or temptation to believe anything but Your Word. Deliver _____ from every bit of evil, pain, weakness, sickness, and lack in their body. For Your kingdom is superior, full of power, full of glory, and for ever and ever You remain the same.

We ascribe all honor, faith, and praise to You, the only one worthy! King Jesus, You are life. In You we live. Breathe the breath of heaven into _____'s lungs and heart today. In Your name, we speak to _____'s body, and we command it to heal up.

Give _____ the new, working, thriving, and strong heart You said You would give if we asked. Jesus, You are the heartbeat we long for. Your presence brings healing. Overshadow _____ today and place Your heart in theirs.

We speak the power of God into that body in Jesus' name. We decree that no fear shall come near you, _____. We call your body into alignment and agreement with the Word of God. Your body must submit to the living, active, and powerful Word of God.

Thank You, Lord. You make all things new. We receive all the works of Your hand and praise You for every breath and every moment of _____'s life. Thank You for being ever present with them and for the comfort that they are never alone.

What a mighty God we serve.

PRAYER:

PRAISES:

DECREE THIRTY-THREE
HE WILL KEEP YOU

May the God of hope fill you with all joy and peace in believing, so that by the power of the Holy Spirit, you may abound in hope (Romans 15:13). We decree an increased power of the Holy Spirit, filling you, _____, with abounding hope that releases joy and peace as you are strengthened in and by the God of all hope.

Today, we lift our eyes to the hills, for our help comes from the Lord, who made heaven and earth. He will not let your foot be moved, _____. Behold, _____, He who keeps you will neither slumber nor sleep.

The Lord is your keeper; the Lord is your shade on your right hand. The sun shall not strike you by day nor the moon by night. The Lord will keep you from all evil; He will keep your life. The Lord will keep your going out and your coming in from this time forth and forevermore (Psalm 121).

Father, today, we hear You speaking _____'s name: (state full name). Your Word says in Isaiah 49:1 that the Lord called you, _____, from the womb, from the body of your mother He named your name. So today, we speak your name, and in doing so, we proclaim your destiny.

_____, we decree you are of nobility because you belong to the family of God, and that makes you noble. You carry the light of Jesus to the world. You cannot be hidden or put under a bucket, but your life will be put on a stand, and you will give light to those around you. Let your light shine to those around you so they may see the works of the Lord and give glory to your Father in heaven (Matthew 5:13-16).

PRAYER:

PRAISES:

DECREE THIRTY-FOUR
EVERLASTING COVENANT

Father, today we stand on Your Word from Genesis 17:7 and Your faithfulness to Your Word that You will establish Your covenant between Yourself and us and our descendants after us in their generations. This is an everlasting covenant for You to be God to us and our descendants after us.

God, we call forth Your faithfulness to fulfill this covenant promise to all our children, our children's children, and generations to come. We thank You for making Yourself known to our grandchildren. Thank You that our children have chosen covenant with You and in faith declare Your faithfulness to their children. Father, we call not only _____ up and into covenantal relationship with You but all of our generational line by faith will come into personal relationship with Your Son, Jesus.

In the name of Jesus, we celebrate every life You have added to our generational line. Today, I rest in Your promise through covenant relationship that the righteous flourish like the palm tree and grow like a cedar in Lebanon. They are planted in Your house; they flourish in Your courts. They shall bear fruit in old age; they are ever full of sap and green, to declare You are upright; You are our rock and there is no unrighteousness in You (Psalm 92:12-15).

We decree today, _____, you shall receive from the blessing of covenant, and you shall flourish and bear much fruit. You shall be a planting of the Lord for the display of His splendor.

Father, we ask that You continue to pour out Your hand of mercy and healing to every part of _____'s being. We praise You for every blessing and touch, for every ounce of provision, and protection over their very life. Thank You for the healing and sustaining You have done and for what is to come.

Thank You for the lavish love You have poured out on us all. Thank You for your empowering grace that has caused us to be steadfast, immovable, and abounding in Your work, for we know that in You, our labor of prayers and faith are not in vain (1 Corinthians 15:58).

We decree today that we shall bless the Lord at all times; His praise shall continually be on our lips (Psalm 34:1). We declare that we trust in the Lord, do good, dwell in the land, and befriend faithfulness. We delight ourselves in the Lord, and He will give us the desires of our hearts.

We declare our ways are committed to You, Lord. We trust in You and believe You will act. You will bring forth Your righteousness as the light and Your justice as the noonday.

We will be still before the Lord and wait patiently for Him (Psalm 37:3-7).

PRAYER:

PRAISES:

DECREE THIRTY-FIVE
INHERIT THE LAND

"Guide me in your truth and teach me, for you are God my Savior, and my hope is in you all day long. Remember, Lord, your great mercy and love, for they are from of old" (Psalm 25:5-6).

"Do not remember the sins of my youth and my rebellious ways; according to your love remember me, for you, Lord, are good. Good and upright is the Lord; therefore he instructs sinners in his ways. He guides the humble in what is right and teaches them his way. All the ways of the Lord are loving and faithful toward those who keep the demands of his covenant. For the sake of your name, Lord, forgive my iniquity, though it is great" (Psalm 25:7-11).

"Who, then, are those who fear the Lord? He will instruct them in the ways they should choose. They will spend their days in prosperity, and their descendants will inherit the land. The

Lord confides in those who fear him; he makes his covenant known to them" (Psalm 25:12-14).

"My eyes are ever on the Lord, for only he will release my feet from the snare. Turn to me and be gracious to me, for I am lonely and afflicted. Relieve the troubles of my heart and free me from my anguish. Look on my affliction and my distress and take away all my sins. See how numerous are my enemies and how fiercely they hate me! Guard my life and rescue me; do not let me be put to shame, for I take refuge in you" (Psalm 25:15-20).

Deliver _____, O God, from all their troubles (Psalm 25:22).

We declare it is the Lord who guides and teaches us His ways. Thank You, Lord, for all Your ways of dealing with us are loving and faithful. Our hope is in You all day long. Remember, O Lord, Your great mercy and love concerning _____ and their healing.

Thank You, Lord, that those who fear Your name will end their days in prosperity and their descendants will inherit the land. We decree You have a portion and land of promise You have reserved for _____ and all their descendants. Because our eyes are ever fixed on You, You will release us from the enemies' snares. We decree You're turning to _____ and are healing every one of their afflictions.

You, God, are restoring and healing the troubles of their physical body in Jesus' name! We praise You for guarding their life and rescuing them.

_____, we speak the refuge of the Lord is your hiding place. We decree the peace and rest of the Lord not only fills your body but your entire being. We continue to speak rest in His healing, for there is healing in His rest. We speak the *shalom* of God to invade every part of your being.

Lord, we ask for expedited healing to _____ in supernatural ways in Jesus' name. God, may _____ experience Your wrap-around love holding them tightly. Jesus, have mercy on _____ as You continue to heal and move.

PRAYER:

_____

_____

_____

_____

_____

_____

_____

PRAISES:

DECREE THIRTY-SIX
WAIT FOR THE LORD

We remain confident of this: _____ will see the goodness of the Lord in the land of the living, we decree and declare you shall wait for the Lord; you will be strong and take heart and wait for the Lord (Psalm 27:13-14).

We praise You, God, for You are doing mighty things to restore and bring into fulfillment and wholeness to _____'s being. For in the shelter of Your presence, You hide _____ from all human intrigues; you keep _____ safe in Your dwelling from every word that does not come forth from Your mouth, Lord. Praise be to the Lord, for you show _____ the wonders of Your love (Psalm 31:20-21).

We declare, _____, be strong and take heart, all our hope is in the Lord (Psalm 31:24 NIV).

Thank You, Lord, for You are _____'s hiding place; You will protect them from trouble and surround them with songs of deliverance (Psalm 32:7). We praise You, God, for Your promise to instruct and teach them in the way they should go; You will counsel them with Your loving eye on them (Psalm 32:8).

Therefore, "We wait in hope for the Lord; he is our help and our shield…In him our hearts rejoice, for we trust in his holy name…May your unfailing love be with us, Lord, even as we put our hope in you" (Psalm 33:20-22).

PRAYER:

PRAISES:

DECREE THIRTY-SEVEN
AS AN OLIVE TREE

Deep calls to deep in the roar of Your waterfalls. All Your waves and breakers have swept over _____. By day, Lord, You direct Your love, at night Your song is with _____ (Psalm 42:7-8).

In God we make our boast all day long, and we will praise His name forever (Psalm 44:8).

But _____ is like an olive tree flourishing in the house of God; they will trust in God's unfailing love for ever and ever. For what You have done we will always praise You in the presence of Your faithful people. And we will hope in Your name, for Your name is good (Psalm 52:8-9).

As I sought the Lord for today's declaration, I sensed his leading to Psalm 52:8. God is raising children in hopes that they will grow and flourish as olive trees in the house of the Lord. Yes! Yes! Yes! The olive tree has so much spiritual meaning from Genesis to Revelation. The olive tree and olive branch are symbols of peace, reconciliation, revival, renewal, and anointing.

The flowering olive tree is a symbol of beauty and abundance, and the slow and hearty growth of the olive tree also implies establishment and peace. The tree's fruitfulness and ability to thrive suggests the model of a righteous person whose children are described as "vigorous young olive trees" around God's table (Psalm 128:3).

Much of what I found we have already been declaring over _____'s very life. So today, Lord, we proclaim that _____ is as an olive tree. In the name of Jesus, they will flourish, thrive, and have deep roots in the house of God. We decree the peace of God is reconciling all things about their being with all things kingdom in Jesus' name.

We declare, in the name of Jesus, _____, you are established, whole, and full of fruitful health and life, and you shall produce beautiful fruit for the Lord. The healing anointing oil of the Holy Spirit is bringing healing, supernatural growth, and development to your entire being. For our hope is in the name of Jesus to bring Him glory.

PRAYER:

PRAISES:

DECREE THIRTY-EIGHT
FEARLESS

Have you not known? Have you not heard? The Lord is the everlasting God, the creator of the ends of the earth. He does not faint or grow weary; His understanding is unsearchable. _____, God gives His power to the faint, and to those who have no might, He increases their strength (Isaiah 40:28-29). In Jesus' name, we call your body to attention to "receive" from the Lord, Himself.

Father, we decree the unsearchable knowledge of God to be released to the caretakers of _____ that they would walk in divine knowledge concerning how to care for them so they exponentially thrive. We decree _____ will walk fearlessly, for You are with them. _____ will not walk in distress, for You are their God. You are strengthening and helping them.

Father, today we give You thanksgiving and praise. We ascribe all honor to King Jesus. Thank You for all You have done and all You are doing and all You will do on behalf of _____'s healing and growth.

Because we are Your children, Your servants, we cling to the promise in Isaiah 44 that reminds us—thus says the Lord, who made you, _____, who formed you from the womb, and will help you. Fear not, God has chosen you. He will pour water on thirsty land and streams on dry ground; He will pour out His Spirit upon you, for _____, God has promised to bless our descendants. They shall spring up among the grass like willows by flowing streams. This one shall say, "I am the Lord's," another will call on the God of Jacob, and another will write on his hand "The Lord's."

_____, we decree you belong to the Lord, and your entire being shall spring forth proclaiming the goodness of God. Your life and healing will be a living testimony of the healing miracle power of Jesus!

PRAYER:

_____

_____

_____

_____

_____

PRAISES:

DECREE THIRTY-NINE
HE DELIGHTS IN YOU

_____, we decree you shall be a crown of beauty in the hand of the Lord, a royal diadem in the hand of your God. You shall no more be termed forsaken, and your land shall not be termed desolate, but you, _____, shall be called God's delight, for the Lord delights in you.

On your walls, _____, God has set watchmen—armies of angels—all day and all night they will not be silent. You who put the Lord in remembrance, take no rest and give God no rest until He establishes _____ and makes them a praise to the earth (Isaiah 62:6-7).

We decree, behold the Lord has proclaimed to the ends of the earth, say to the daughter or son, behold, your salvation comes. Behold, His reward is with Him and His recompense before Him. _____, you shall be called the redeemed of the Lord, and He has sought you out (Isaiah 62).

You are His, and His salvation has come to you. Healing, complete restoration, and wholeness are in His hands—we decree to your entire body. Be healed and whole in Jesus' name. We speak to your lungs and declare the strength and breath of God fill you and strengthen you to function at full capacity. We speak the heartbeat of heaven into the chambers of your heart and the affections of God's love for you to overtake you.

PRAYER:

PRAISES:

DECREE FORTY
FORTY TO FORTY-ONE

I can't believe this is declaration forty. As I began to press into what the Lord would have us to speak and to declare today, I couldn't shake a vision of the Israelites wandering in the dessert for forty years, but year forty-one looked much different. The promise was fulfilled. Oh, what a difference one day made.

Noah and his family watched for forty days and forty nights as the rains covered the earth. But on day forty-one, the heavens closed up, and the rains ceased. Noah and his family, tucked inside the very Word of God, were being protected and carried by faith in the words God spoke. Those words God spoke to Noah became the tangible ark in which Noah and his family rode to safety.

The ark, spoken into existence by the mouth of God, became a physical manifestation of Noah's faith in the words God said and Noah's faith, put in action, actually built what God spoke.

Day forty-one came, and the skies cleared up. God remembered Noah, and the ark floated safely on the face of the waters.

Jesus was led into the wilderness and after fasting forty days and forty nights, He spoke, "It is written, man shall not live on bread alone, but on every word that comes from the mouth of God" (Matthew 4:4). And at the end of the test, day forty-one, Scripture says angels came and ministered to Him.

So today, our decree is simple—do it again, God. By faith, we decree day forty-one is a crossover day for _____, a day full of peace and promise, a day You are releasing ministering angels to minister to _____, to restore, heal, and miraculously attend to them in very personal and tangible ways.

We call forth the light of Jesus to engulf _____. God, we are asking for and decreeing a miracle to tangibly form in _____'s body and life in Jesus' name.

We decree that we are anticipating and expecting big things on day forty-one. We call forth the finished work of the cross over and into all Your promises You have spoken in and over _____'s life.

We praise You, God, for all the provision, all the sustaining, all the preparations, and all You have healed to this point, and we stand decreeing, the Word of God heals you, _____!

PRAYER:

PRAISES:

DECREE FORTY-ONE
ABOUND IN HOPE

Father, today we take great peace in knowing You have spoken many things concerning _____, and therefore, our peace is found in You. We take heart because we know You have overcome everything in the natural that may try to hinder _____'s victories (John 16:33).

We decree the victories of God in every area of wholeness to your body, _____. We declare You will flourish and abound in perfect peace and health (Psalm 72:7). We decree Jesus purchased your complete healing, _____ (Isaiah 53:5).

Thank You, Lord, that _____ can both lie down and sleep, for You alone, O Lord, make them dwell in safety (Psalm 4:8). Today, we are reminded of every wound You suffered and endured on _____'s behalf.

God, today we declare that we believe every word You speak. Thank You that because Your written Word is alive and active, Your Word is present tense as Holy Spirit breathes fresh life to those words there on the page. We believe You have spoken, You are speaking, and You continue to speak Your Word and promises.

We believe You; this is why we know that You, the God of all hope, are filling us with joy and peace in believing, so that by the power of the Holy Spirit, we may abound in hope (Romans 15:13).

And the peace of God, which surpasses all understanding, will guard your hearts and minds in Christ Jesus (Philippians 4:7). _____, we declare the tangible peace of God will be like a protective device you wear that is preventing injury or damage to your heart and mind. The Prince of Peace, Himself, is watching over you to guard and protect against any harm in Jesus' name.

God, we thank You for protecting _____ with Your peace as you lead them into the promises You alone fulfill. Thank You for keeping them safe as they rest upon every word You have spoken to their life and destiny. Thank You for keeping them secure in the ark of Your love.

We decree mercy, peace, and love are multiplied to you, _____, and you shall be fruitful and multiply (Jude 1:2).

PRAYER:

PRAISES:

DECREE FORTY-TWO
HIS GREATNESS

God, we decree You are not only good, You are great! Yours, O Lord, is the greatness, power, glory, victory, and majesty. Indeed, everything that is in the heavens and the earth, You have dominion over. O Lord, You are exalted as head over all (1 Chronicles 29:11).

We declare Your greatness is head over everything concerning _____'s care and progress. We speak Your dominion to be present in that atmosphere. The atmosphere of Your kingdom rules and reigns, not only in that room but within their entire being. We continue to call forth the peace and rule of God to inhabit _____'s body in Jesus' name.

_____, we speak to your lungs and decree complete strength, wholeness, and renewal, just as God designed. The righteous right hand of God is upon your very being, molding, shaping, and forming you to completion and perfect health. We call forth victories to manifest at the sound of the promises and words of God.

We decree doctors, nurses, and caretakers to align with the progress and wisdom of God for your care. We speak no unnecessary testing or poking in Jesus' name. And when tests are necessary, the results bring confirmation of God performing miracles on your behalf to bring glory to His greatness. We proclaim to Him, who alone does great wonders, for His lovingkindness is everlasting (Psalm 136:4).

God, we decree today that we believe You still perform wonders and signs that point to who You are as the God who does what is impossible for man. We are asking for expedited healing, growth, and wholeness.

_____, you are not bound to the timetable of man. You are free to partner with your creator to heal at the speed of His Word spoken over you. We decree, _____, you will not conform to the pattern of this world but will be transformed by the renewing of your mind. Then you will be able to test and approve what God's will is—His good, pleasing, and perfect will (Romans 12:2).

We ask that those working with _____ would not conform to the patterns of the world but their minds would be flooded with the power and creativity of God in their care of _____, bringing about supernatural results.

We ask, Lord, that You would keep all stress, anxiety, and fear far from _____. They are surround by Your steadfast love that penetrates every ounce of their being in Jesus' name. We decree that Your steadfast love never ceases over _____. Your mercies for _____ never come to an end. They are new every morning, for great is Your faithfulness to _____ (Lamentations 3:22-23).

We speak to any hint of infection, be gone in Jesus' name. We release the pure and powerful blood of Jesus into _____'s body that burns away any and all unclean sources trying to invade.

_____, we decree your body is the temple of the Holy Spirit, and no defilement can trespass on holy ground in Jesus' name. We rejoice in this day, for great is the Lord and greatly is He to be praised.

PRAYER:

PRAISES:

DECREE FORTY-THREE
SONGS OF PRAISE

Shout for joy to the Lord, all the earth. Worship the Lord with gladness; come before Him with joyful songs. Know that the Lord is God. It is He who made you, _____, and you are His.

We are His people and sheep of His pasture. We will enter His gates with thanksgiving and His courts with praise. We shall give thanks to Him and praise His name. For the Lord is good and His love endures forever; His faithfulness continues through all generations (Psalm 100).

Father, we shout praise to You for Your faithfulness in keeping _____. We sing songs of praise for You are such an awesome shepherd who watches, protects, and cares for Your lambs. Father, we declare today, You are sending Your light and Your faithful care to lead them to Your healing presence, to the very place You dwell (Psalm 43:3). Our hope is in You, Lord.

We decree, Lord, Your ways are holy. There is no god as great as You. You are the God who performs miracles; You display Your power among the peoples. With Your mighty arm, You are redeeming them (Psalm 77:13-15). God, we appeal to heaven and ask for a mighty healing miracle to move in _____'s life in Jesus' name!

PRAYER:

PRAISES:

DECREE FORTY-FOUR

WELL WITH YOUR SOUL

_____, we declare that your body is a temple of the Holy Spirit within you, whom you have from God. You are not your own, for you were bought with a price. We decree, _____, you will glorify the name of God in your body, today (1 Corinthians 6:19-20).

_____, we pray that all will go well with you and that you will be in good health, as it goes well with your soul (3 John 1:2). We are asking for a miraculous touch of Jesus and for the power of Jesus to go forth and make you well and strong (Luke 8:46).

We declare our trust is in the Lord, and with all our heart, we don't lean on our own understanding. In all our ways we declare that we acknowledge Him, and He will make our paths straight.

We are not wise in our own eyes, for we fear the Lord and turn away from evil. Therefore, we stand on the promise that every word God speaks will be healing to your flesh and refreshment to your bones (Proverbs 3:5-8).

We proclaim the joy of the Lord is strengthening you, _____, as we stand in faith, believing God is for you.

We rejoice in You, God, for You are mighty to save and full of love and grace.

PRAYER:

PRAISES:

DECREE FORTY-FIVE
YOU ARE

_____, we pray that out of God's glorious riches, He would strengthen your lungs with the power of His Spirit in your inner being so that Christ may dwell in your heart through faith. We decree you are being rooted and grounded and established in the Father's love for you (Ephesians 3:16-17).

Father, we decree the truth, for without faith it is impossible to please You, because anyone who comes to You must believe You exist and that You reward those who earnestly seek You (Hebrews 11:6). We are standing in faith, believing who You are—You are the God of the impossible. You are the God who restores and rebuilds. You heal and help in our times of need. You comfort and carry. You are the God of the "no chance" and the "slim chance" and the "far out there, fat chance."

You still make all things possible. We believe You still part waters, move mountains, multiply fish and loaves, walk on the waves, and calm storms. You still make all things new, call dead things to life, perform signs, miracles, and wonders. All this is not just what You do, it's who You are! You are true to Your nature.

Today, we decree we believe You. Therefore, we also take You at Your word that You, Yourself, will reward those who seek You. Lord, You said to ask believing and what we ask shall be done. We decree we will not walk in doubt. We will not be blown or tossed about. Our confidence is in You, the Lord of miracles (James 1:6).

Father, we are confident that You have heard every prayer lifted on behalf of _____, and we thank You that You have heard every one of them.

We believe we will see the glory of God. Today, we decree the very words of Jesus to you _____. _____, "Come out of that hospital." We decree to all the machines and tubes and medicines, "Unbind _____ and let them go!" _____, you are free to move and live and praise the name of Jesus.

You are called to freedom. Out of our distress we called to the Lord on your behalf, _____, and He answered and has set you free (Psalm 118:5).

By the authority and anointing of Jesus, we proclaim liberty and freedom from all machines, medicines, and tubes, and we call your body into the fullness of health and healing purchased for you, _____, by the precious blood of Jesus.

PRAYER:

PRAISES:

DECREE FORTY-SIX
VICTORIOUS ONE

Father, we decree today that You alone are the way, the truth, and the life. In You, we find everything we need. Thank You, God, that You care for and love your children. You, God, are called the victorious one. You, God, have never known defeat.

So we decree today, _____, you cannot be anything other than victorious in your battles, for He who overcame the world lives in you (John 16:33).

You, _____, are called an overcomer. You shall overcome any struggle, obstacle, or barrier that stands in the way of abundant life in Jesus. In all these things, we are overwhelming conquerors through Him who loves us (Romans 8:37).

We decree today that you are not just conquering, but you will overwhelmingly conquer every challenge, marker, machine, ungodly word, doubt, or barrier that rises up against the whole, full, abundant, and flourishing life God planned for you before you took your first breath.

You are loved with an everlasting love that holds all power to conquer darkness, weakness, sickness, and lack. _____, the Word of God says, whatever is born of God (that's you) is conceived from the Father. He has formed and fashioned you. We decree in agreement with the Word that what is born of God overcomes the world because of Jesus' victory over death, hell, and the grave. It is our faith in the victory of Jesus that propels us to victory (1 John 5:4-5).

"Jesus," we shout, "You, are the Son of God, and in You is all authority, power, and glory!" You alone rise with healing in Your wings (Malachi 4:2).

_____, we decree over you, go forth, break free from the stall. For the great physician Himself, King Jesus, is covering you. He shall bring healing and restoration to your entire being. Rest in His healing.

PRAYER:

_____

_____

_____

_____

_____

PRAISES:

DECREE FORTY-SEVEN
BEYOND MEASURE

Father, today we shout, "Great is our Lord, and abundant in power; His understanding is beyond measure!" (Psalm 147:5). We decree that You alone know and understand all things. Continue to show us Your ways and bring greater revelation to who You are.

We confess, there is so much more of Your wisdom to understand, more of Your power to witness, and more of Your love to encounter. You have been infinitely kind and generous and powerful in Your dealings with _____.

We decree that You are endlessly creative; therefore, we continue to petition heaven for Your majestic touch to miraculously strengthen and restore _____ to full health and wholeness.

_____, we decree today that you are not dependent on man, machine, or medication; your dependency is in every miracle, prophecy, and word of God for your life.

When we look to the heavens, the works of God's fingers, the moon, and stars, which You, God, have set in place, what is man that You are mindful of him (Psalm 8:3-4)?

We decree the fingers of God, the place where He releases His power, has created your entire being, _____, and we give Him praise today, for His thoughts toward you are good, and His plans for you are for your future and hope.

Even every hair on your head, _____, has all been accounted for by your heavenly Father. He knows what you need before we even ask, so fear not for you are of more value than many sparrows (Luke 12:7). We decree that we will seek first the kingdom of God, and our God, knowing exactly what you need, _____, will provide for you according to His good pleasure (Luke 12:31-32).

PRAYER:

_____

_____

_____

_____

PRAISES:

DECREE FORTY-EIGHT
ESTABLISHED IN PROMISE

Lord, today we decree that Your faithfulness and love endure forever. You are _____'s rock and fortress, and for Your name's sake, You are leading and guiding them. You have taken them out of the net that was set for them. You alone are their refuge. Into Your hands we commit _____'s spirit, body, and soul; for You have redeemed them, O Lord, our faithful God (Psalm 31:3-5).

We decree that the Word of the Lord is upright. All Your work is done in faithfulness (Psalm 33:4). Great are Your works, God, and we delight in everything You have done. Full of splendor and majesty are the displays of Your mighty hand at work in _____'s life.

Thank You for Your hand of grace and provision in providing

miraculous care for _____. Because You remember Your covenant with us, You bring forth provision. The works of Your hand are faithful and just, and Your Word is trustworthy and established in Your promise of fulfillment.

Father, we decree that we eagerly anticipate today to be a big crossover into the fulfillment of every promise You have spoken over _____'s life. This is the day You have made, and we rejoice.

PRAYER:

PRAISES:

DECREE FORTY-NINE
ARM OF THE LORD

We decree today that you, _____, are like a tree planted by streams of water, and your body is yielding its good fruit in season. You do not wither, and all you do prospers, for the Lord watches over all your ways (Psalm 1). The strong right arm of the Lord is raised in triumph concerning you. The strong right arm of the Lord has done glorious things (Psalm 118:16).

We join with all creation and shout, "Ah, Lord God, it is You who have made the heavens and the earth by Your great power and by Your outstretched arm—nothing is too hard for You!" (Jeremiah 32:17).

_____, there is nothing concerning you that is too big for God to triumph over. Our hope and trust is in the Lord. In His hand is the life of every creature and the breath of all mankind (Job 12:10). We declare that you are in the best hands. God is holding all things together (Colossians 1:17). _____, rest in knowing God's strong and mighty hands are holding you, and He will never let go.

PRAYER:

PRAISES:

DECREE FIFTY
JEHOVAH RAPHA

Today, we decree there is only one Jehovah Rapha—one God who heals.

"L<small>ORD</small> my God, I called to you for help, and you healed me" (Psalm 30:2). We praise you for who you are God. You are _____'s healer. We are calling on You to deliver _____ from dependency on any machine or medication to assist them. You said if we called upon You for help, You would heal. Thank You for Your healing touch. Thank You, God, for meeting all _____'s needs according to the riches of Your glory in Christ Jesus (Philippians 4:19).

Beloved, _____, we pray that all may go well with you and that you may be in good health, as it goes well with your soul (3 John 1:2).

Father, we long for the day of _____'s deliverance from the tubes, machines, and medications. We believe you can strengthen, heal, and make all things new. We ask, would you do it quickly? Increase _____'s strength. We speak the power of Your words to make them whole and strong and new in Jesus' name. "LORD, be gracious to us; we long for you. Be our strength every morning, our salvation in time of distress" (Isaiah 33:2).

PRAYER:

PRAISES:

ABOUT THE AUTHOR

Sherrie has been teaching the Word of God since 1981 and in full-time ministry since 2002. As an associate pastor at Beltway Park Church in Abilene, Texas, she develops, coordinates, and teaches adult Bible classes under the umbrella of "Beltway Freedom." As associate pastor of freedom, Sherrie operates in pastoral care as well as training and equipping the saints in the areas of freedom, healing, prophecy, and prayer ministries.

Her ministry activates believers to hear the voice of the Lord and releases strategies to win spiritual battles. She travels nationally and internationally, imparting, in her transparent style, truth that sets the captive free, turning them from darkness to light. She is instrumental in leading leaders by equipping them with freedom material and tools to impart to others in their regions and churches.

The specific call on Sherrie's life comes from Acts 26:17-18, "…I am sending you to them to open their eyes and turn them from darkness to light, and from the power of Satan to God, so that they may receive forgiveness of sins and a place among those who are sanctified by faith in me."

Sherrie and her husband, Dirk, have been married since 1981 and serve together in overseas missions to Ireland. They are the parents of four grown children and the proud grandparents of thirteen. In 2019, Sherrie authored *JT's Ups with Downs, When Life Hands You Down Syndrome There's Only One Way Up*. Sherrie loves everything outdoors and anything related to her grandchildren. When not in the Word, you can find her in nature or observing her beloved chickens.

SherrieSaltzgaber.com

ENDNOTES

1 "Decree Definition & Meaning." *Dictionary.com*, Dictionary.com, https://www.dictionary.com/browse/decree.

Made in the USA
Middletown, DE
14 March 2023

26750906R00096